TOP TRADE CAREERS

LANDSCAPE DESIGNER

A Crabtree Branches Book

Kelli Hicks

CRABTREE
Publishing Company
www.crabtreebooks.com

School-to-Home Support for Caregivers and Teachers

This high-interest book is designed to motivate striving students with engaging topics while building fluency, vocabulary, and an interest in reading. Here are a few questions and activities to help the reader build upon his or her comprehension skills.

Before Reading:
- *What do I think this book is about?*
- *What do I know about this topic?*
- *What do I want to learn about this topic?*
- *Why am I reading this book?*

During Reading:
- *I wonder why...*
- *I'm curious to know...*
- *How is this like something I already know?*
- *What have I learned so far?*

After Reading:
- *What was the author trying to teach me?*
- *What are some details?*
- *How did the photographs and captions help me understand more?*
- *Read the book again and look for the vocabulary words.*
- *What questions do I still have?*

Extension Activities:
- *What was your favorite part of the book? Write a paragraph on it.*
- *Draw a picture of your favorite thing you learned from the book.*

TABLE OF
CONTENTS

IN MY COMMUNITY

Many people work in a community. An ambulance driver takes injured people to the hospital quickly.

An electrician works with the wires in your home to make sure that the lights will turn on, and that your gaming system has the power it needs for you to play your favorite game.

Some people help to make your community beautiful. Have you ever heard of a landscape designer?

A landscape designer is a person who plans what plants and flowers, water features, lighting, and trees will make outdoor spaces that are attractive and **functional**.

WHAT DO I NEED?

Are you artistic and able to handle several tasks at the same time? You might be a great landscape designer. To get started, you need a high school diploma. Landscape designers must also have a two-year or four-year college diploma or degree.

While in school, students choose a path to study landscape design, **horticulture**, plant science, or biology. In some places, designers are required to have a license.

Are landscape designers and landscape architects the same? They are similar. However, designers tend to focus on smaller projects for homes while architects often take larger projects for public spaces or businesses. Landscape architects generally have more education or higher degrees.

SPECIAL SKILLS

Landscape designers need a special set of skills. Designers need to be creative, but also have strong attention to detail.

They need to have excellent communication skills to understand what the **client** wants and to be able to explain the challenges of each project.

Designers also need to be able to look at the natural and human-made **elements** of the area. They need to understand types of soil and how to make the water drain properly.

They need to understand which types of plants grow best in the sun or in the shade. They also know the types of plants that grow best in the areas where they will be planted.

Landscape designers need to have computer skills. Most use technology to plan for the area that needs to be improved.

They also need to be able to create and manage contracts and maintain **budgets**, so math skills are a must.

Many landscape design companies use social media to grow their businesses. Designers post pictures of completed projects and show the before and after of the jobs. Future clients can get ideas for what they want to have in their yards.

Landscape designers sometimes work for a company or they can be self-employed.

The designers spend part of their time in an office meeting with clients or using computer design **software**. They spend the rest of their time visiting the outdoor locations where the designs will be created.

First, the landscape designer meets with the client and visits the area that needs improvement. Together, they talk about the **scope** of the project and what the client wants. Then, the designer takes pictures of the project location.

The designer analyzes the current area to create a plan. The designer makes a drawing or uses computer technology to figure out what the final area will look like.

The designer makes a list of the plants that are necessary. The plan identifies the exact location for each plant, the placement of the lighting, and the method for keeping the plants watered.

The designer hires a **crew** to do the work on the project. The designer supervises the crew and manages the project to make sure everyone follows the plan.

Some areas of the country are very dry and need designs that require little water. Grass needs a lot of water, so designers use plants native to dry areas instead. They also use mulch to hold water or stone for design.

Landscape designers need to be environmental experts. They need to create designs that are **sustainable**, selecting the right plants for each job.

They also try to install sprinkler and watering systems that do the best job of conserving water. They have a responsibility to protect the environment.

Landscape designers often use solar-powered lights instead of electrical lights in projects. Solar lighting usually costs less and conserves energy.

NOT ALWAYS EASY

There are some challenges in this job. If you select the wrong plants for the soil type, the plants will not live. It takes time and money to complete the needed classes.

It can be difficult to provide what the client wants within the given budget. Water shortages and climate change can make the design process more difficult as well.

MAKING A LIVING

Landscape design can be a **rewarding** career. Not only can you help people, but you can earn a good living as well.

Your salary may be affected by where you live, your level of experience, and whether you work for someone else or for yourself.

Landscape Designer	$28,000 - $62,000
Landscape Architect	$63,000 - $120,000
Horticulturist	$35,700 - $119,000
Landscape Crew	$22,000 - $35,000

Landscape designers are important community workers. They create beautiful spaces for people to enjoy, and can use their special skills to show care and respect for the environment.

GLOSSARY

budgets (BUHJ-its): plans for how money will be earned or spent

client (KLY-uhnt): someone who pays for the services of another

crew (KROO): a group of people who work together

elements (EL-uh-muhntz): the basic, simple parts of something

functional (FUHNGK-shuh-nuhl): something that works well or is designed to work well

horticulture (HOR-tuh-kuhl-chur): the growing of fruits, vegetables, and flowers

rewarding (ri-WOR-ding): something that gives you pleasure and satisfaction

scope (SKOHP): a range of opportunity

software (SAWFT-wair): computer programs

sustainable (suh-STAYN-uh-buhl): capable of being kept up or maintained over time

INDEX

WEBSITES

www.landscapeindustrycareers.org/discover-the-industry/career-paths/landscape-designer

www.zippia.com/landscape-designer-jobs

www.thespruce.com/difference-between-landscape-architect-and-designer-2736682

ABOUT THE AUTHOR

Kelli Hicks

Kelli Hicks is a teacher and writer who lives in Florida with her family. She loves having colorful flowers as an invitation for beautiful butterflies to fly through the landscape of her backyard.

CRABTREE
Publishing Company

Written by: Kelli Hicks

Designed by: Jennifer Dydyk

Edited by: Tracy Nelson Maurer

Proofreader: Ellen Rodger

Print and production coordinator: Katherine Berti

Photographs: Cover career logo icon © Trueffelpix, diamond pattern used on cover and throughout book © Aleksandr Andrushkiv, cover photo © Pressmaster, photo of drawing tools on cover and title page © Toa55, Page 4 top photo © OgnjenO, bottom photo © Tyler Olson, Page 5 © Pixel-Shot, Page 6 © Artazum, Page 7 © Toa55, Page 8 © Iakov Filimonov, Page 9 top photo © ProStockStudio, bottom photo © Gorodenkoff, Page 10 © Toa55, Page 11 © Lucky Business, Page 12 top photo © New Africa, bottom photo © Billion Photos, Page 13 © Joanne Dale, Page 14 top photo © Virrage Images, bottom photo computer on desk © BongkarnGraphic, image on computer screen © kanesuan saksangvirat, Page 15 © GaudiLab, Page 16 inset photo © Have a nice day Photo, background photo © Hywit Dimyadi, Page 17 © Pressmaster, Page 18 © SpeedKingz, Page 19 top photo © Africa Studio, bottom photo © Supa Chan, Page 20 © Lamyai, Page 21 top photo © Will478, bottom photo © Bill Florence, Page 22 top photo © Toa55, bottom photo © Dragon Images, Page 23 top photo © Virrage Images, bottom photo © Grisha Bruev, small inset photo © Bizoner, Page 24 © Production Perig, Page 25 top photo © Brett Hondow, bottom photo © fizkes, Page 26 inset photo © GaudiLab, background drawing © charobnica, Page 27 © Lyubov Levitskaya, Page 28 top photo © Scott E. Feuer, bottom photo © Lilly Trott, Page 29 top photo © Toa55, bottom photo © Viacheslav Lopatin. All images from Shutterstock.com

Library and Archives Canada Cataloguing in Publication

Available at the Library and Archives Canada

Library of Congress Cataloging-in-Publication Data

Available at the Library of Congress

Crabtree Publishing Company

www.crabtreebooks.com   1-800-387-7650

Copyright © 2022 **CRABTREE PUBLISHING COMPANY**

Published in the United States
Crabtree Publishing
347 Fifth Avenue
Suite 1402-145
New York, NY, 10016

Published in Canada
Crabtree Publishing
616 Welland Ave.
St. Catharines, ON
L2M 5V6

Printed in Canada/082022/CPC20220818